TYPES OF PLANTS

MADDIE GIBBS

Britannica®
Educational Publishing

IN ASSOCIATION WITH

ROSEN
EDUCATIONAL SERVICES

Published in 2019 by Britannica Educational Publishing (a trademark of Encyclopædia Britannica, Inc.) in association with The Rosen Publishing Group, Inc.
29 East 21st Street, New York, NY 10010

Distributed exclusively by Rosen Publishing.
To see additional Britannica Educational Publishing titles, go to rosenpublishing.com.

First Edition

Britannica Educational Publishing
J.E. Luebering: Executive Director, Core Editorial
Mary Rose McCudden: Editor, Britannica Student Encyclopedia

Rosen Publishing
Bailey Maxim: Editor
Nelson Sá: Art Director
Nicole Russo-Duca: Designer & Book Layout
Cindy Reiman: Photography Manager
Ellina Litmanovich: Photo Researcher

Library of Congress Cataloging-in-Publication Data

Names: Gibbs, Maddie, author.
Title: Types of plants / Maddie Gibbs.
Description: New York : Britannica Educational Publishing, in Association with Rosen Educational Services, 2019. | Series: Let's find out! Plants | Includes bibliographical references and index. | Audience: Grades 1–4.
Identifiers: LCCN 2017053521| ISBN 9781538302019 (library bound) | ISBN 9781538302026 (pbk.) | ISBN 9781538302033 (6 pack)
Subjects: LCSH: Plants—Juvenile literature. | Plants—Classification—Juvenile literature. | Botany—Juvenile literature.
Classification: LCC QK49 .G48 2019 | DDC 580—dc23
LC record available at https://lccn.loc.gov/2017053521

Manufactured in the United States of America

CONTENTS

WHAT ARE PLANTS?

What do a sweet-smelling rose bush, a tall oak tree, and an insect-eating Venus flytrap have in common? They are all plants. In fact, these are just three of the many, many types of plants in the world.

Like animals, plants are living things. However, there are many differences between plants and animals. Unlike animals, plants cannot move around. Plant cells are different from animal cells, too.

The Venus flytrap is a plant that traps and eats insects. It belongs to a group of carnivorous, or meat-eating, plants.

They have stiff walls made of a tough material called cellulose.

While animals need to eat food to survive, almost all plants make their own food. They do this using a process called photosynthesis. Photosynthesis requires sunlight, chlorophyll, water, and carbon dioxide, which is a gas. Chlorophyll is a substance in all green plants, especially in the leaves. Plants take in water from the soil and carbon dioxide from the air.

Chlorophyll is in the green parts of plants, such as the leaves and stems of this fern.

TREES, SHRUBS, AND HERBS

Plants can be classified in several ways. To classify things means to place them in different categories, or groups. A common method of classifying plants is based on their growth form. Plants are called trees if they have tall, woody stems, or trunks, and are generally 8 feet (2.4 meters) or more in height when they are full-grown. Shrubs are low, woody plants, usually with many stems branching off close to the ground. Herbs have tender, juicy stems in which the woody tissue

Baobab trees have thick trunks. They are found mainly in Africa.

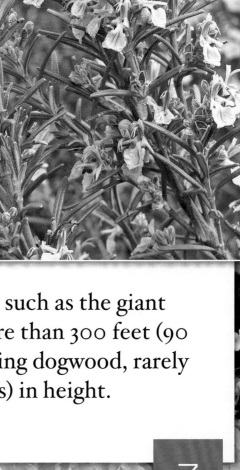

COMPARE AND CONTRAST

How are shrubs like trees and herbs? How are they different?

Rosemary is an herb. It is native to the Mediterranean region, where it still grows wild.

is much less developed than it is in shrubs and trees.

Within each of these groups there is a great deal of variety. For example, some trees, such as the giant sequoia, can grow to heights of more than 300 feet (90 meters). Others, such as the flowering dogwood, rarely grow to more than 30 feet (9 meters) in height.

How Complex Is That Plant?

Scientists organize the plant kingdom into divisions that are arranged in order from the simplest to the most complex. The plant divisions can be arranged into three main groups based on differences in their structure. These groups are the nonvascular plants, seedless vascular plants, and vascular seed plants.

◄◄ Vascular plants have roots, stems, and leaves. Roots hold a plant in the ground and take in water and food.

VOCABULARY

Vascular describes living things that have structures like tubes or channels to carry fluid (like the blood of an animal or the sap of a plant).

There are more than nine thousand species, or types, of liverworts.

Vascular plants have special tissues, called xylem and phloem, that carry water and food throughout the plant. Vascular plants also have roots, stems, and leaves. Vascular plants include herb plants, shrubs, and trees. Most vascular plants produce seeds. They use the seeds to reproduce. Plants that do not have seeds use cells called spores to reproduce.

Nonvascular plants do not have xylem or phloem. They also lack true roots, stems, and leaves. Nonvascular plants include mosses, liverworts, and hornworts. They are generally small and grow in moist places.

Nonvascular Plants

The first land plants were the liverworts, hornworts, and mosses. These nonvascular land plants first grew more than 450 million years ago. They are the simplest kinds of plants. Some of these plants can survive in dry habitats, but they all need a lot of moisture to reproduce.

Liverworts have simple stems or sometimes no stems

Green mosses often grow on trees, forest floors, and rocks.

at all. They have either simple leaves or flat green bodies that resemble leaves. On their undersurfaces are rootlike structures but no true roots. Hornworts have small green bodies that are flat and almost circular. The spore cases are capsules that rise slightly above the surface of the plants—these are the "horns" of the hornworts. Mosses show the beginnings of leaves, stems, and roots. They were the first green plants to stand upright.

THINK ABOUT IT

Why were the mosses the first green plants to stand upright? What features do they have that might help them do that?

Hornworts are a group of small nonvascular plants that favor damp, shady habitats in warm environments.

Seedless Vascular Plants

Seedless vascular plants first appeared on Earth more than 400 million years ago. Seedless vascular plants include the club mosses, horsetails, and ferns. These plants have stems, roots, and leaves that are similar to those of seed-producing plants. However, they reproduce by means of spores.

Club mosses are usually a few inches high, though their stems may grow along the ground for more than

Horsetails grow in moist, rich soils in all parts of the world except Australasia. They are also known as scouring rushes.

COMPARE AND CONTRAST

How are seedless vascular plants like nonvascular plants? How are they different?

50 feet (15 meters). They have small scalelike leaves and look like little pine trees. Horsetails have jointed stems that look like bamboo. The scaly leaves grow in whorls around the stem at the joints. Club mosses and horsetails have spore-producing cones at the tops of their branches.

Millions of years ago the ancestors of the modern ferns covered Earth in vast forests. Tropical ferns still grow as tall as trees. In temperate climates, ferns are generally small, shade-loving plants.

Ferns can be recognized by the featherlike shape of their leaves, which are called fronds.

VASCULAR SEED PLANTS

Seed plants evolved more than 300 million years ago. Vascular seed plants include conifers and flowering plants. They have xylem and phloem. Plants that reproduce by means of seeds do not need a lot of moisture in order to complete their life cycle. As a result, seed plants can grow in much drier habitats than plants that depend on spores for reproduction.

Seed plants include five divisions: cycads, ginkgophytes, conifers, gnetophytes, and flowering plants. The first four groups are called gymnosperms, a

All fruit-bearing trees, such as this orange tree, are flowering plants.

name that means "naked seed." It refers to the fact that their seeds are exposed on the scales of cones. Members of the last division, flowering plants, are called angiosperms. The seeds are protected inside a structure on the plant.

Millions of years ago, cycads were among the most abundant plants on Earth. Today they are found only in wet tropical forests. These plants look like palm trees.

THINK ABOUT IT

Plant types that evolved more recently are more complex. Why do you think that is?

> Ginkgos are very hardy trees. They resist damage from insects and fungi, plantlike living things that sometimes grow on trees.

The ginkgo tree is often called a living fossil. It is the only surviving species of ginkgophyte. It originally grew only in China. Now ginkgo trees are planted in many parts of the world.

Gnetophytes have many features that resemble those of flowering plants, but they have naked seeds. This small division has about 100 members.

Conifers are common in the world's temperate forest ecosystems. Most conifers produce pollen and bear their

VOCABULARY

Pollen is the substance that causes plants to form seeds. New plants then can grow from the seeds.

seeds in cones. These cones vary in size from less than 0.5 inch (1.3 centimeters) around in junipers to nearly 2 feet (0.6 meter) long in sugar pines. Most conifers are evergreen. That means that they keep their needlelike leaves year-round. Several conifers, however, such as the larch and bald cypress, shed their needles during the harsh winter months. Some conifers, such as the yellowwood of the Southern Hemisphere, have broad leaves.

These cones are on a larch tree. Larches grow mainly in cool areas in the northern half of the world.

FLOWERING PLANTS

The first flowering plants appeared several million years after the first conifers. The reproductive structures of these plants are flowers, and their seeds are protected within a fruit. More than 300,000 species of flowering plants have been described, more than all other kinds of plants combined.

The flowering plants were once divided into two groups—monocots and dicots—based on how their seeds sprout. Sprouting monocots produce

Arrowheads are monocots. They grow in shallow lakes, ponds, and streams.

These flowering plants are eudicots. The word "eudicot" means "true dicot."

a single leaf. Newly sprouted dicots produce two leaves.

Modern studies have showed scientists that the dicots are actually two groups, basal dicots and eudicots. Monocots and basal dicots evolved first and have important similarities. Eudicots came later.

THINK ABOUT IT

Plants have been around longer than people. Why do you think scientists are still learning new things about them?

Most monocots are herbs; they include such plants as grasses, lilies, and orchids. Not all monocots are small, however. Palm trees, for example, may grow to more than 100 feet (30 meters) in height.

The basal dicots include a variety of herbs, shrubs, and trees. Water lilies, star anise, laurels, and magnolias are just a few examples of plants in the basal dicot group.

The eudicots are the largest group within the angiosperms and include a wide variety of

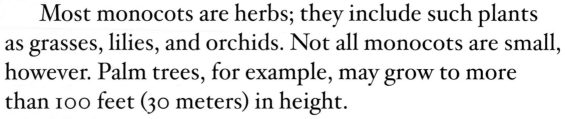

Star anise is the dried fruit of the *Illicium verum*, an evergreen tree and basal dicot. It is used as a spice in cooking.

herbs, shrubs, and trees. Eudicot trees include oaks, maples, beeches, and hickories. Familiar eudicot herbs include roses, asters, carnations, buttercups, and tulips. Most food crops also are eudicots, including cabbages, potatoes, apples, kale, peanuts, and beans. An exception is corn, which is a grass and therefore a monocot.

THINK ABOUT IT

Why do you think that most of the crops people use for food are eudicots rather than monocots or basal dicots?

The stately beech is a popular tree in many regions of the world. People plant beeches for their shade and their colorful leaves.

ANNUALS AND BIENNIALS

Flowering plants are often divided into three groups, according to the length of their life cycles. Annuals complete their life cycle in a single year. The seeds sprout, the seedlings develop into flowering plants, new seeds are produced, and the parent plant dies—all in a single growing season. Annual plants often grow in habitats with harsh conditions during part of the year. They survive through such times in the form of seeds.

Zinnias are perennial in places where they are native but annual elsewhere.

COMPARE AND CONTRAST

How are biennials like annuals? In what ways are they different?

Many garden flowers, such as zinnias and pansies, are annuals.

Biennials need two years to complete their life cycle. In the first year they produce stems and leaves. In the second year they produce blossoms and seeds and then die. During the first year they store up the food that they need to produce flowers and seeds the following year. Garden flowers in this group include foxgloves and hollyhocks.

Foxgloves are native to Europe, the Mediterranean region, and the Canary Islands.

23

PERENNIALS

Perennials live for more than two years—sometimes for centuries. The oldest individual tree on Earth is thought to be a bristlecone pine that is more than five thousand years old. Wildflowers are perennial plants. Garden perennials include peonies, irises, and phlox.

Some perennials produce flowers and seeds throughout their lives. Others produce flowers only once and then die. The American aloe, for example, lives for more than a decade while its stem and leaves

Moss phlox is a perennial herb that blooms each spring. It is also called mountain phlox and moss pink.

grow. Eventually, it produces a flowering stalk up to 40 feet (12 meters) tall. After the flowers mature and seeds are produced, the plant dies.

Most perennials are annual above ground—that is, their stems, leaves, and blossoms die in the fall. These plants, however, survive through the winter by means of their underground roots and stems. Trees, shrubs, and herbs also live and grow in much the same way.

THINK ABOUT IT

If you were planting a garden, what kinds of flowering plants would you want?

Forsythia is a perennial bush. There are several species, some of which bear yellow flowers in early spring.

BIODIVERSITY

Plants can be found wherever there is sunlight, air, and soil. On the northernmost coast of Greenland, the Arctic poppy peeps out from beneath the ice. Mosses and tussock grasses grow in Antarctica. Flowers of vivid color and great variety force their way up through the snow on mountainsides. Many shrubs and cacti thrive in deserts that go without rain for years at a time. Rivers, lakes, and swamps are filled with water plants.

The main plants in tussock grasslands, like this one in New Zealand, are tussock grasses. They grow in cool, moist places.

The Amazon rainforest contains several million species of insects, plants, birds, and other forms of life.

The variety of animal and plant life in any environment is known as biodiversity. The term can apply to a small portion of a particular rainforest, the entire Earth itself, or any habitat in between. The many types of plants on Earth contribute to biodiversity in a big way. Biodiversity is of special interest to those concerned with the environment and the study of living things.

THINK ABOUT IT

Rainforests are known for their great biodiversity. Why do you think that is?

The great variety of plants and animals is often taken for granted. However, some of the things that people do, such as cutting down rainforests, pose a major threat to the environment.

Consider the changes that happen when a new housing development is built. If a forest is transformed into a neighborhood of streets, lawns, and houses, the old environment and the habitat it provided for living creatures changes forever. The environment is disrupted or even destroyed. Most of the plants will be ruined. The animals that eat those plants will be forced either

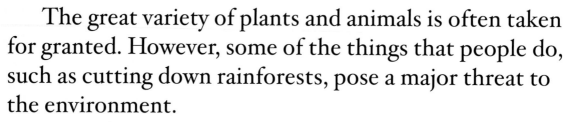

When large forests are cut down, the biodiversity of the area is greatly reduced.

VOCABULARY

A species becomes **extinct** when there are no longer any members of that species alive.

to find a new habitat or die. Sometimes an entire species might become extinct.

Because Earth is the only place in the universe known to sustain life, the loss of even one species on the planet means the total loss of that species.

This model is of a plant species that went extinct long ago. While species have always died out, humans are making that process happen faster.

GLOSSARY

abundant Existing in large numbers.

blood vessels A system of tubes that carry the blood throughout the body.

carbon dioxide A colorless gas. People and other animals breathe out carbon dioxide, while plants need it to make food.

chlorophyll A green pigment that plays an important role in photosynthesis.

climate The weather found in a certain place over a long period of time.

conifer A member of a group of trees and shrubs that produce cones.

crops Plants that people raise for food.

ecosystem All the living and nonliving things that occur together within a particular area.

environment All the physical surroundings on Earth.

evolved Developed over time from an earlier form.

habitat The place where a living thing or a community of living things lives.

life cycle A series of changes that happens to all living things. Every life cycle is the same for every generation.

photosynthesis The process in which green plants use sunlight to make their own food.

reproduce To make more of one's own kind.

root Part of a plant that is usually hidden underground. Roots hold the plant in the ground and keep it upright.

seedling A newly sprouted plant.

species A specific type of living thing. Human beings are a species.

sustain To keep something going.

temperate Having mild weather, often changing with the seasons.

tissue A group of cells that work together to do a specific job.

tropical Having hot weather year-round and being near the equator.

whorl A row of similar parts (such as leaves or petals) in a circle around a point.

FOR MORE INFORMATION

Books

Amstutz, L. J. *Investigating Plant Life Cycles* (Searchlight Books What Are Earth's Cycles?). Minneapolis, MN: Lerner Publishing Group, 2015.

Holmes, Porter. *Plants in My Pond* (Plants in My World). New York, NY: PowerKids Press, 2018.

Ingoglia, Gina. *The Tree Book for Kids and Their Grown-Ups*. Brooklyn, NY: Brooklyn Botanic Garden, 2013.

Rattini, Kristin Baird. *National Geographic Readers: Seed to Plant*. Washington, DC: National Geographic Kids, 2014.

Stewart, Melissa. *A Seed Is the Start*. Washington, DC: National Geographic Kids, 2018.

Terrazas, April Chloe. *Botany: Plants, Cells and Photosynthesis* (Super Smart Science). Austin, TX: Crazy Brainz Publishing, 2014.

Websites

Better Homes & Gardens
http://www.bhg.com/gardening/plant-dictionary
Twitter: @BHG, Facebook: @mybhg, Instagram: @betterhomesandgardens

National Wildlife Federation
https://www.nwf.org/en/Garden-for-Wildlife/About/Native-Plants/Native-Plant-Types
Twitter: @NWF; Facebook, Instagram: @NationalWildlife

USDA
https://plants.usda.gov

INDEX